READ ALOUD
SHIVA TALES
Bhasmasura's Boon
............and other Stories

Author
VANEETA VAID

READ ALOUD

SHIVA TALES
Bhasmasura's Boon
............and other Stories

Nita Mehta Publications
Enriching Young Minds

Nita Mehta Publications

Corporate Office
3A/3, Asaf Ali Road, New Delhi 110 002
Phone: +91 11 2325 2948, 2325 0091
Telefax: +91 11 2325 0091
E-mail: nitamehta@nitamehta.com
Website: www.nitamehta.com

© Copyright NITA MEHTA PUBLICATIONS 2013
All rights reserved
ISBN 978-81-7676-105-5

First Print 2013

Printed in India at Infinity Advertising Services (P) Ltd, New Delhi

Editorial and Marketing office
E-159, Greater Kailash II, New Delhi 110 048

Typesetting by National Information Technology Academy
3A/3, Asaf Ali Road, New Delhi 110 002

Distributed by :
NITA MEHTA BOOKS
3A/3, Asaf Ali Road, New Delhi - 02

Distribution Centre :
D16/1, Okhla Industrial Area, Phase-I,
New Delhi - 110020
Tel.: 26813199, 26813200
E-mail: nitamehta.mehta@gmail.com

Contributing Writers:
Subhash Mehta
Tanya Mehta

Editorial & Proofreading:
Rajesh
Ramesh

WORLD RIGHTS RESERVED: The contents - all text, photographs and drawings are original and copyrighted. No portion of this book shall be reproduced, stored in a retrieval system or transmitted by any means, electronic, mechanical, photocopying, recording or otherwise, without the written permission of the publishers. While every precaution is taken in the preparation of this book, the publishers and the author assume no responsibility for errors or omissions. Neither is any liability assumed for damages resulting from the use of information contained herein.
TRADEMARKS ACKNOWLEDGED: Trademarks used, if any, are acknowledged as trademarks of their respective owners. These are used as reference only and no trademark infringement is intended upon.

Price: Rs. 145/-

CONTENTS

Introduction   7

The Day Lord Shiva Drank Deadly Poison   8

Shiva Visits Little Krishna   13

Bhasmasura's Boon   19

Plague Tricks Nandi   25

Shiva Goes to War!   30

How Shiva Married Parvati?   37

Activities   44

INTRODUCTION

The most powerful of Hindu Gods is considered to be Lord Shiva. It is said that Lord Brahma creates everything that is born, Vishnu preserves it and Shiva helps in recreating by destroying the old to bring in the new. Lord Shiva is married to Goddess Parvati. They have two children, Ganesha and Kartikeya. Shiva smears ash all over his body and wears garlands of snakes! He lives at Mount Kailash, in the frozen terrains of the Himalayas! This book carries entertaining stories about Shiva that children are definitely going to enjoy.

THE DAY LORD SHIVA DRANK DEADLY POISON

One day, Lord Shiva was praying. Suddenly, he heard this call, "Help us Lord Shiva, help us!"

Earlier the Gods and demons had been churning an ocean. A mountain was placed in the middle on the ocean. A five headed snake was used as the churning rope. Lord Vishnu turned himself into a tortoise and balanced the mountain on his back. Now why would they be doing that? That is because underneath the ocean, there were rare treasures!

Amongst the treasures was the great healer, Dhanvantri. He held the jar containing the nectar of immortality (living forever).

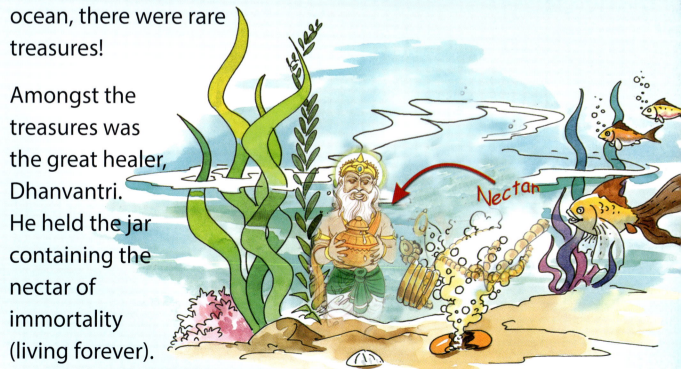

Oh dear! Whilst churning the ocean, a poisonous pot of gases came up!

The deadly poison choked everyone. That is why they desperately called for Shiva.

Lord Shiva immediately rushed to help.

Lord Shiva snatched the poisonous pot and drank the contents. This way no harmful gases remained. Everyone was safe. Oh no! The poison was so toxic that it burnt Lord Shiva's throat. Lord Shiva fell down unconscious.

The Moon watching from above, beamed cooling rays on Shiva's throat. The Moon's cool rays healed the effect of the poison. Soon, Lord Shiva awoke. But the effect of the poison had made Shiva's throat blue. From that day, Shiva came to be known as 'Neel Kanth' or the blue throated one.

Shiva thanked the Moon for helping him. The Moon replied humbly, "I am glad I could be of some help to you, Lord. If I had my way, I would always stay with you."

Shiva granted the Moon's request and the Moon got a permanent place on the side of Shiva's forehead.

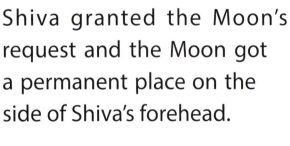

SHIVA VISITS LITTLE KRISHNA

Lord Vishnu came to visit Lord Shiva one day. "I am going to earth in the form of a baby," Lord Vishnu informed him. "Why?" asked Shiva. "Well there is great evil happening on earth. I plan to live and grow up on earth for a while and fix things. My name is going to be Krishna!" said Lord Vishnu.

"I really want to see you in the form of a baby! I shall come to earth to meet you," promised Lord Shiva.

After some days, Shiva decided to meet his friend on earth. Shiva transformed himself into a 'Sadhu' (ascetic).

Whoosh

Now as a Sadhu, Shiva made his way to earth and reached the address Vishnu had given him.

On arrival, Shiva knocked. "Who is it?" a lady called Yashodha came out. There was no baby in her arms. Shiva curiously asked her to bring her baby out so he could bless the baby. "My baby will be scared seeing a stranger. I will not bring him out!" refused Yashodha.

Suddenly, the baby began to cry. Yashodha ran inside.

Shiva closed his eyes and mentally spoke to Vishnu. Vishnu was the baby, who was crying. "Vishnu I have come to meet you. But your mother is not allowing me to!" Vishnu immediately answered, "Don't worry. I have a plan."

"WWWWWAAAAAAAAH!" Baby Krishna cried louder. Yashodha rushed to pick him up. He kept crying. Yashodha just could not comfort him.

She stepped out of the door with Krishna. That is when Shiva saw his friend in the form of a baby! When Yashodha was not looking, Krishna nodded at Shiva.

Whoosh

Happily, Shiva returned home. Krishna suddenly stopped crying too.

BHASMASURA'S BOON

Bhasmasura was a king who wanted to be very powerful. He prayed for many, many days to Lord Shiva.

Pleased, Lord Shiva reached the praying Bhasmasura. "What boon do you want?" Shiva asked Bhasmasura.

"I want to be so powerful that if my right hand touches anyone's head, be it a man, a demon or even a God, they should turn to ash," boomed Bhasmasura.

Lord Shiva was so pleased with Bhasmasura that he unthinkingly granted his wish!

"Aaaaargh!" Bhasmasura began touching heads of his enemies. One by one, they all turned to ashes. Wild with power, Bhasmasura confronted Shiva, "I plan to touch you!"

Horrified by this attack, Shiva fled. Shiva sadly realized he had foolishly granted a very powerful wish to Bhasmasura! He had put himself in harm's way by doing so!

Shiva ran up the mountains with Bhasmasura chasing him. Somehow giving Bhasmasura a slip, Shiva ran further up.

There he met lord Vishnu. Shiva hurriedly told him everything. "Quick, hide in that cave!" suggested Vishnu.

"Vishnu help me"

As soon as Bhasmasura reached, instead of Shiva, he met a beautiful fairy. Fascinated, he stared at her.

The fairy was dancing.

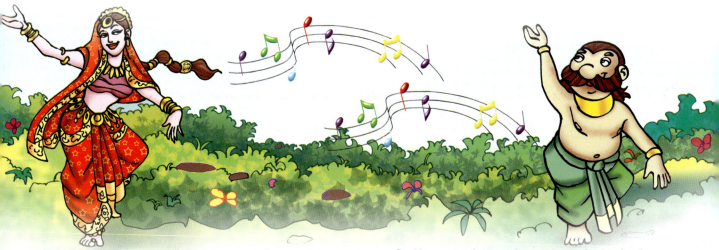

Bhasmusura began to dance too! He followed each step she did. If she threw one hand on one side, he copied her. If she threw the other hand there, he copied her again.

The fairy raised her right hand and touched her head. So did Bhasmasura.

"SWOOOOOOOOOSH" he turned into a pile of ash! He had been tricked into destroying himself!

The fairy was actually Lord Vishnu. He saved Lord Shiva. A very embarrassed Lord Shiva came out of the cave and gratefully thanked lord Vishnu for his help.

PLAGUE TRICKS NANDI

One day, the king of Bijapur begged Shiva to help him fight the dreaded disease called Plague. Plague was threatening to attack Bijapur.

"Take Nandi, my most trusted bull, to Bijapur. He will guard your kingdom against Plague," advised Shiva.

On Shiva's orders, Nandi guarded the kingdom of Bijapur.

So when Plague rushed to attack Bijapur, Nandi stopped him. "Aaaaargh, let me in!" growled Plague.

"No!" Nandi bellowed.

Plague attacked Nandi! Oh dear, a very big fight started! They fought day in and day out!

Soon Nandi and Plague were tired. "All right. I will let you enter Bijapur if you promise to make only one person ill," said Nandi.

Plague agreed, nodding eagerly.

Nandi shrugged and gave Plague a pass. Oh dear, Plague cheated. It made hundreds of people ill instead of only one person!

Nandi realized Plague had tricked him. With a roar he attacked Plague.

Bifff-bash-bang!

He beat Plague up.

"Helppppp!" Plague ran away. It never returned to Bijapur ever again!

SHIVA GOES TO WAR!

One day, all the Gods came to Shiva and begged him to fight the three demon brothers. "But why?" Shiva asked.

"These powerful demon brothers have made life impossible for us. They have boons from Lord Brahma. Only you have the power to fight with them and destroy them!" cried the Gods.

Demon brothers attacking the Gods

"But I do not have a chariot or a bow and arrow!" said Shiva.

"I will make you a chariot, a bow and arrow!" offered Vishwakarma, the architect of the heavens.

"Very well!" Shiva agreed to help.

Vishwakarma made a beautiful golden chariot. He then made a sturdy strong bow and arrow. The bowstring was going to be 'Sheshnag' the poisonous serpent (snake)! Shiva's quiver (arrow container) was filled with arrows made from lightening!

"I will be your charioteer!" declared Lord Brahma.

Finally, Shiva sat on his chariot. He looked at all the Gods and gently said.

"These brothers are demons. Yet somewhere they have some goodness in them. But then why are they being so bad?"

The Gods could not find an answer. So Shiva said, "This is because they are allowing the animal or brute that resides in every one's soul to control them. That is why they have become savages."

The Gods nodded.

"To win this war, I need you to give me all the brutes or animals inside each of you. These brutes make you angry and wild. They make you fight the war. You must give them up. Once we destroyed the demons, we will make sure life will always be peaceful."

The Gods happily agreed. Shiva chanted a prayer. Do you know what happened? Every God suddenly transformed into the savage animal he was allowing to live within his soul. There were tigers, wolves, bears, elephants and many other animals everywhere!

Shiva took command of all the animals. With one look he tamed them. By this action he became 'Pashupatinath' or the God of the animal kingdom. He signaled to Brahma to take him to the demons.

Shiva reached the three palaces of the demons. He stood on his chariot and aimed his bow. With one strong movement he pulled the bow. Twanggggggggggg! Showers of lightening arrows sped towards the demon abode.

Phsssssssssss-swapppppppppppp-thuk thuk thuk!

The arrows found their aim and destroyed all three palaces and killed the three demon brothers.

"Hail Shiva!" every one rejoiced.

HOW SHIVA MARRIED PARVATI?

Parvati really wanted to marry Lord Shiva.

Sadly, he was not aware of her at all! He would sit in prayer on top of frozen mountains with his eyes closed. Poor Parvati. She sat right next to him and he never seemed to see her!

However, unknown to Parvati, Shiva did notice her. But he never let her know.

'I need to test Parvati. I need to check whether she will make me a fitting wife,' thought Shiva.

So, one day, he disguised himself as a 'Sadhu'. Coming towards Parvati, he scoffed at her saying "Stop running after Shiva, the filthy beggar,"

Parvati was so angry at the Sadhu's words that she lost her temper.

"Don't you dare call Shiva names. He is the greatest amongst all Gods!"

Shiva was pleased with her answer. He changed his form. Parvati blushed when she saw that the 'Sadhu' was actually Shiva.

Shiva came to marry Parvati with wedding guests that were, ghosts, spirits, snakes and wild animals! Shiva himself was dressed in animal skin and garlands of snakes.

Parvati's mother was so scared seeing all these strange guests and the way Shiva was dressed. Parvati requested Shiva to change his form for the wedding.

Shiva transformed himself into a handsome groom and Parvati's mother was happy seeing him! It was beautiful wedding and the Gods and Sages showered many blessings over the couple!

COLOUR IMAGE OF SHIVA WITH THE SUGGESTED COLOURS

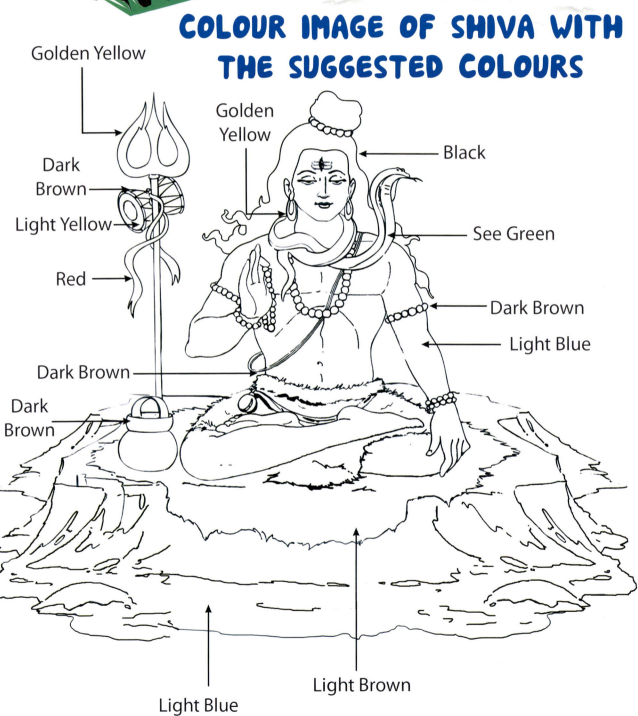

Did You Know?

 Why Shiva wears tiger skin? Because the tiger is considered to be one of the most ferocious of beasts. By wearing its skin, Shiva claims total power over the wild forces of nature.

 Why Shiva has a third eye? Because he is all seeing. That is his eye of wisdom and knowledge. Shiva opens his third eye only to destroy the evils threatening existence.

 Why Shiva has deadly cobra coils wrapped three times around his neck? The coils stand for time. Past, present and future. This shows even though the existence of life depends on time, Lord Shiva has controlled time and is above it too!

Simple Crossword Puzzle

Across:
1. .... (5) is Shiva's bull.
2. Shiva drank the .... (5) poison.

Down:
3. .... (7) opened the door and met Shiva who was disguised as a Sadhu.
4. .... (5) lives on Mount Kailash.

Answers: 1. Nandi, 2. Deadly, 3. Yashodha, 4. Shiva

HELP SHIVA REACH THE CAVE TO ESCAPE BHASMASURA

FIND THE HIDDEN WORDS IN THE GRID

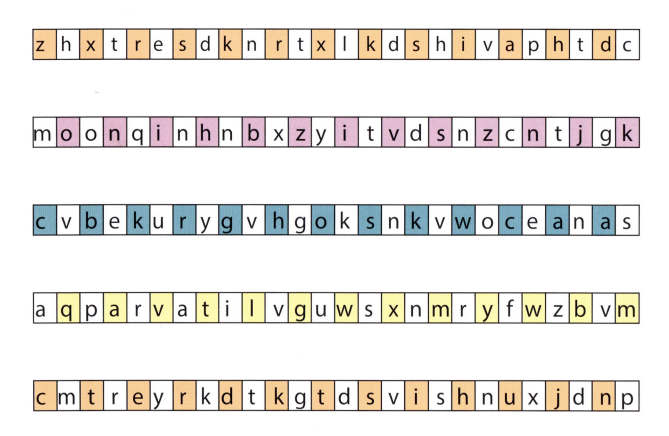

Answers: Shiva, Moon, Ocean, Parvati, Vishnu